MARLBOROUGH
IN OLD PHOTOGRAPHS
A SECOND SELECTION

THE LONDON ROAD looking north towards St Mary's church in 1894.

MARLBOROUGH
IN OLD PHOTOGRAPHS
A SECOND SELECTION

—————— COLLECTED BY ——————
PAMELA COLMAN

ALAN SUTTON

Alan Sutton Publishing
Phoenix Mill · Far Thrupp · Stroud · Gloucestershire

First Published 1990

British Library Cataloguing in Publication Data

Marlborough in old photographs: a second selection
1. Wiltshire. Marlborough, history
I. Colman, Pamela
942.317

ISBN 0–86299-759–8

Front cover Illustration:

THE MAURICE FAMILY of Marlborough with their gypsy caravan in the yard at Lloran House, High Street, in about 1895. The man wearing a bowler hat is Cox, the coachman.

Typeset in 9/10 Korinna
Typsetting and origination by
Alan Sutton Publishing
Printed in Great Britain by
Dotesios Printers Limited

CONTENTS

VIEW OF HIGH STREET in around 1850.

INTRODUCTION

It has always seemed to me legitimate to collect photographs, pictures and engravings for their subject matter rather than their artistic merit, for their historical and topographical interest, and this collection has been assembled almost entirely with this fact in mind, though I hope it is not without some artistic interest. They offer eloquent glimpses of the enthusiasms of our predecessors and reflect the great width of their interests, which however ephemeral at one time have now acquired the patina of age.

The old town of Marlborough and the college which now carries its name into every quarter of the globe are unquestionably under great mutual obligation to one other. Certainly the former has the latter to thank for coming to its rescue following the collapse of the great coaching days. The history of the place takes us back to prehistoric times however. The Castle Mound, a gigantic tumulus in the grounds of Marlborough College, is similar to its even greater neighbour some half a dozen miles to the west, the famous Silbury Hill. The old Roman station of Cunetio lies a mile to the east; and not far from here the remarkable Iron Age 'Marlborough Bucket', now preserved in the Museum at Devizes, was found in 1807.

Marlborough is pictorially remarkable for its wide, sloping High Street springing from the college gates in the west and stretching for over half a mile towards the east above the banks of the River Kennet. Photographs can show us the town at the height of its stage coach activity, when it was a major stopping place on the famous London to Bath road, its decline following the arrival of the railways, and how quiet the Marlborough streets were before the development of the petrol engine in the period 1900 to 1930.

Marlborough has two fine churches, St Peter's and St Mary's. Their stonework and grand proportions contrast with the domestic architecture of the more prosperous citizens, whose homes were of wood and brick, and even more with the houses of the bulk of the townspeople in the alleys running back from the High Street. The Tudor Reformation destroyed the chantry chapels and vestiges only remain, most notably the Priory in the High Street.

The prosperous citizens of a growing town would require a charter enabling them to control (to some extent) their own affairs, and municipal activity is illustrated, along with inns and shops. We can glimpse a little of the part played by Marlborough in the two World Wars, and an interesting map used by a German bomber crew (probably on their way to bomb the railway yards at Swindon) in 1940 is included. The universal love of the 'outdoors' and of games and their place in the life of Marlborough are featured in a section on recreation. Finally, Marlborough has had its share of literary figures: Louis MacNeice, John Betjeman, Siegfried Sassoon, Charles Sorley, and Sir Edward Hilton Young, later Lord Kennett, who wrote,

But I was born in Marlborough
And love the homely faces there
And for all other lands beside
'Tis little love I have to share.

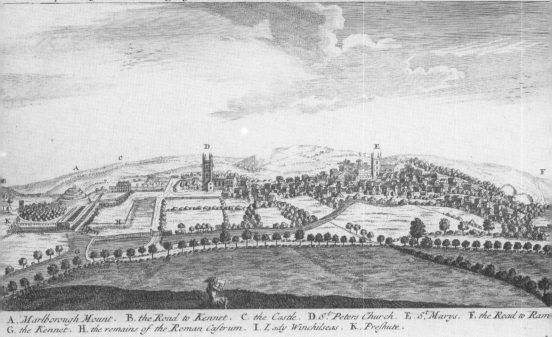

A. *Marlborough Mount.* B. *the Road to Kennet.* C. *the Castle.* D. *St Peters Church.* E. *St Marys.* F. *the Road to Ram*
G. *the Kennet.* H. *the remains of the Roman Castrum.* I. *Lady Winchilseas.* K. *Preshute.*

THE TOWN in 1723 as it appeared to the antiquarian, William Stuckley.

Growth of the Town

The first Ordnance Survey map shows the High Street with St Mary's church to the east and St Peter's and the early buildings of Marlborough college to the west. The London or Great Bath Road enters from the east through the parish of Preshute. The two mills and their mill streams are shown. The gardens behind the houses on the south of the High Street run down to the river Kennet, crossed by Duck's bridge, London Road bridge and 'Stone bridges'.

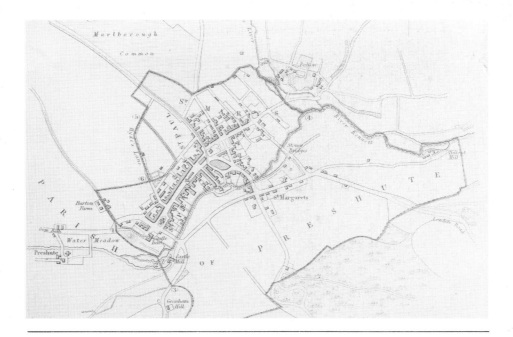

THE HIGH STREET LOOKING EAST in 1840.

THE MARLBOROUGH BUCKET, an Iron Age burial vessel and fine example of celtic art, decorated with human heads and strange animals. It is attributed to the age preceding the Roman occupation.

THE PREHISTORIC MOUNT, OR CASTLE MOUNT, above, is of archaeological interest, as is its larger neighbour Silbury Hill, below. The photograph is of about 1870 and the road is the present A4. The Mount was terraced early in the seventeenth century as part of the pleasure grounds of the Seymour mansion, which now forms part of Marlborough College.

TWO VIEWS OF THE HIGH STREET. The lock-up, town pump and weighbridge are in the foreground in the top, older, picture and can still be seen in the later view, below; the colonnading extends some distance on the north of the street.

THE GREEN photographed from an oil painting of about 1750.

THE GREEN viewed from the east before 1830, from a painting in the Town Hall. The white house with twin gables behind the lime trees was the early home of the novelist William Golding, son of a master at the college.

TWO VIEWS OF ST MARTINS from the Green. Gas lit the streets until 1929.

THE PRESENT TOWN HALL being built by C.E. Ponting at the eastern end of the High Street in 1901. Behind it lies St Mary's church.

ST PETER'S is at the western end. Marlborough has the distinction of a fine church at each end of the High Street.

AN AERIAL VIEW TAKEN in 1951 showing the development of the stable-yards, workshops and cottages behind the High Street façade.

HIGH STREET & TOWN HALL, MARLBOROUGH.

MARLBOROUGH HIGH STREET is one of the most picturesque of English rural high streets. It stretches its generous breadth directly eastwards for half a mile. No town in England has quite so ample a main thoroughfare.

PART OF THE STREET presents rather an unusual appearance. A colonnade projecting before shop windows serves as a promenade for pedestrians in bad weather.

LONDON ROAD LOOKING NORTH, C. 1900.

JUNCTION OF LONDON AND SALISBURY ROADS. The pleasant gas lamp-standard has been replaced by a mini-roundabout. The 7th Wiltshire war memorial stood here once.

GEORGE LANE runs parallel with the High Street on the Kennet side. It retains the row of interesting Elizabethan cottages.

GEORGE LANE looking east to London Road in July 1924.

STREETS BY THE TOWN HALL. High Walls (or New London Road, left,) was built to ease coach traffic coming up the narrow Parade (below).

The Parade. Marlborough.

THE KING'S MILL, now demolished, below the college on 'Treacle Bolly'. The name is said to derive from the miller's pony and to have been adopted by generations of boys at the college for their 'College Bolly' pudding.

THE TOWN MILL, demolished in 1950. The site is now a housing development although the mill stream still exists.

STONE BRIDGES, an early crossing point on the Kennet to the east of the town.

POULTON BRIDGE over the River Og.

AT THE CORNER of Kingsbury Street and Silverless Street is a fine gabled house, which with others in the latter street survived the fire of 1653. Most of the buildings in Kingsbury Street are seventeenth-century with plaster fronts over timber frames.

THE DORMY HOUSE, as it was called, for many years an antique shop on the corner. It is a fine example of a Jacobean building.

SALISBURY ROAD JUNCTION, c. 1910.

POULTON HOUSE, built in 1706. The most perfect house in Marlborough.

KINGSBURY STREET looking north, C. 1900.

Kingsbury Street, Marlborough.

THE SAME STREET looking south.

HIGH STREET under snow in the winter of 1910.

Herd Street, Marlborough.

HERD STREET was still traffic-free in 1900. The high curb still exists today.

SOME OF THE MANY CARS stuck in snow during the severe winter of 1963.

HIGH STREET looking west in the '50s. Note reconstruction on the left after a fire at Dible and Roy, furnishers. The white building beyond was once a cinema, now a supermarket.

LLORAN HOUSE at 42 High Street. The doctor's house, before the Victorian addition. Once the site of the Cock Inn this was the home of the Maurice family for 130 years.

LLORAN HOUSE with the Victorian addition to the left and entrance to the doctor's surgery beyond. The Georgian porch has now been removed.

LLORAN HOUSE from the rear. Extensive gardens stretched down to the Kennet.

THESE DWELLINGS, Nos 96–98 High Street, were pictured in a sale catalogue of 1922. All this property has now been developed.

THE HIGH STREET, C. 1950. Free's furniture van stands outside Herd and Leader's garage, the Polly Restaurant (white façade, right) still has its upper floors.

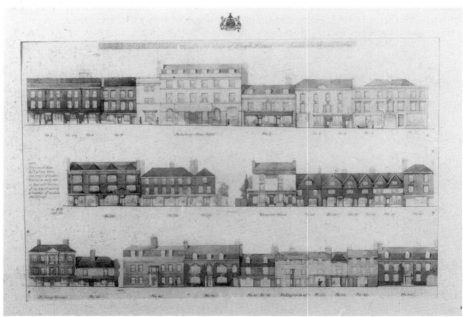

THE SOUTH SIDE OF THE HIGH STREET in 1939, before the Second World War, made as a record should bombing destroy the town.

Castle to College

This print encapsulates the story of what is now the site of Marlborough College. In the right foreground is the prehistoric mound used by the Normans as the foundation for the keep of their castle, no trace of which remains today. In the centre is the elegant mansion the Seymours built in the early eighteenth century, with its stable courtyard and St Peter's church on the left. The River Kennet is in the background. The mansion became the fashionable Castle Inn on the Old Bath Road, and is now part of Marlborough College.

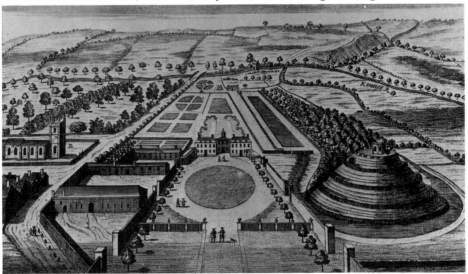

THE CASTLE INN, famous in the eighteenth century as a fashionable coaching establishment. The painting by George Manton is from around 1840. The house built by the Seymours c. 1700 became an inn in 1751. By the 1830s the landlord kept 400 horses to draw 40 coaches a day on the Hungerford to Marlborough and Marlborough to Devizes stages. In 1836 the Halcomb family, coach masters, foresaw the probable result of the railways on their business and helped promote the change from inn to college.

AN IMAGINARY SCENE showing coaches outside the Castle Inn. A reproduction of a late Victorian painting.

THE SOUTH SIDE of the same building, now a boarding house of the college.

THE COLLEGE in the 1850s. There was much new building between 1843 and 1848 and one of the first buildings to be erected was the chapel.

BISHOP COTTON, Master of Marlborough College between 1852 and 1858 and subsequently Metropolitan of India. Also shown are the upper school, the chapel and the staircase of the old inn.

COLLEGE COURT IN 1862. Trees were planted as an avenue from gate to porch two years later. Black caps and jackets were compulsory uniform.

THE COLLEGE, above in 1865 and below in 1873. The tradition is that 'Mr Duck was ready to dispense tuck from his barrow'.

VOSS, THE COLLEGE PORTER, with wife and daughter outside the Porter's Lodge, c. 1866. The school bell is above the porch.

PORTER SHEPPARD OUTSIDE THE NEW LODGE. With a pair of binoculars he could read the cricket scoreboard on the pavilion and record the progress of the game on the lodge noticeboard.

MR J.R.H. O'REGAN WITH A CLASS, C. 1900. In 1902 the poet Siegfried Sassoon, then aged fifteen, was in his form Shell A. Pat O'Regan, Balliol scholar, Irish hockey international and senior history master who taught at the college for twenty-eight years, was very popular and much respected. Sassoon wrote in later life 'he was so easy to work for' and 'sometimes he read us a little poetry . . . and would tell us to write some ourselves', with a prize of half-a-crown for the best. 'Thank you Mr O'Regan for those half-crowns'. Sassoon's prize-winning verses, which O'Regan framed and hung in the classroom, concluded:

> *but extra lessons cannot kill*
> *and blows are not so hard*
> *that they will end the life of this*
> *ambitious little bard.*

THE MASTER OF THE COLLEGE, Canon G.C. Bell (seated centre front) with his bursar, the Revd J.S. Thomas on his right (standing). The master held his appointment for twenty-seven years and the bursar for forty-seven. Of the former, Siegfried Sassoon, who was at the college from 1902 to 1904, said that he looked so venerable that it would be difficult for him to be anything else.

THE UPPER SCHOOL, built in 1846 and demolished in 1937, from an etching by E.M. Holman. This room would be crowded by 120 boys.

RUGBY PLAYERS AT THE COLLEGE GATES, c. 1930.

SIR ASTON WEBB'S FIELD HOUSE AND BRIDGE in 1911.

THE COLLEGE COMMEMORATION OF ITS FOUNDERS, c. 1910, an annual Sunday affair. The Friday and Saturday were prize days and social occasions.

PRIZE DAY CROWDS pass through the college gates.

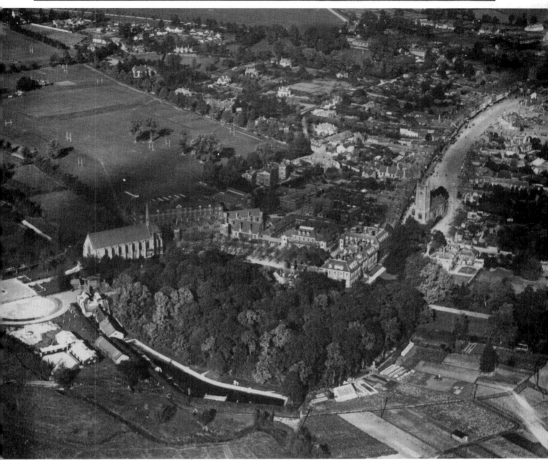

AN AERIAL VIEW OF THE COLLEGE in 1922. The Mount is screened by trees. All that remains of the castle moat is the college bathing place. The foundations of the War Memorial Hall about to be built are clear (left background). The High Street is open and there are no parking problems.

CANON BELL, THE MASTER, with Major General Kekewich CB, Old Marlburian, at the unveiling of the South Arican War memorial on 23 March 1903. The Bishop of Salisbury is in attendance.

SECTION THREE

Churches
and
Chapels

Marlborough today has two very fine churches, one at either end of the High Street. St Mary's at the eastern end is the parish church, and St Peter's to the west is now the headquarters of the St Peter's Trust and an information centre, although services may still be held there. Churches in Marlborough are mentioned in 1091 and 1223, St Mary's, St Peter's and Preshute (half a mile to the east) being included. St Mary's was rebuilt in Tudor times, burnt out in the disastrous fire of 1653, and rebuilt again partly with money ordered to be collected by Oliver Cromwell. Though considerably repaired in the last 150 years it is basically the church rebuilt by the Cromwellians. St Peter's escaped the 1653 fire, and is in its general plan much the same as it was when built in 1460. Puritanism and nonconformity were strong in Marlborough from the seventeenth century onwards. The Roman Catholic church is modern and stands on the site of the old George Inn.

ST PETER'S FROM THE EAST. This water-colour by John Buckler shows the church before the Victorian restoration. Cardinal Wolsey was ordained here in 1498.

ST PETER'S FROM THE WEST. A Perpendicular church of good stone restored in 1862. The tower is 120 ft high with very heavy pinnacles.

ST MARY'S in 1805 from a water-colour by Buckler. The pinnacles were considered to be dangerous and were removed around 1800.

THE SOUTH SIDE OF ST MARY'S, the parish church of the town, restored in 1844. The building was gutted in the 1653 fire and re-roofed.

ST PETER'S CHURCH INTERIOR fitted with fine box pews. Nowadays it houses the Tourist Information Centre and other secular activities having been taken over by the St Peter's Trust in 1978.

THE ROOF UNDER REPAIR by the St Peter's Trust.

THE FIRST CHAPEL OF MARLBOROUGH COLLEGE, built in 1848 from plans by Edmund Blore. It was demolished in 1884 to make way for the present larger chapel.

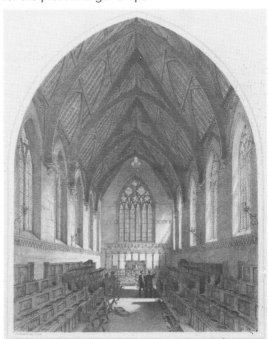

THE FIRST COLLEGE CHAPEL INTERIOR from a print by E.H. Buckler (published by A. Emberlin of Marlborough).

THE SECOND COLLEGE CHAPEL, built in 1886 to designs by Bodley and Garner, is 154 ft long and 54 ft wide. It is dressed with Bath stone in the Perpendicular style. The four niches in the apse have been filled with figures of St George, St Patrick, St Andrew and St David, presented by tradesmen connected with the town.

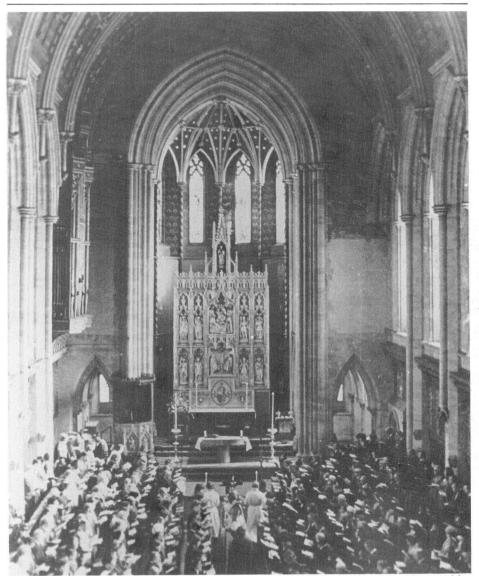

INTERIOR OF THE COLLEGE CHAPEL. The glass in one of the south windows was designed by Burne-Jones and crafted by William Morris, an early pupil at the college. In 1951 Sir Ninian Comper restored the chancel.

ST MARY'S INTERIOR. The arcading is Cromwellian. The church interior was greatly damaged by the fire of 1653. It was restored in 1844 and the chancel was only added in 1874.

ST PETER'S INTERIOR before the box pews were removed. Note the hanging rail with vestments.

ST GEORGE'S CHURCH, PRESHUTE, is a Victorian rebuild, but it has an interesting thirteenth-century font, which, according to tradition, came from the castle.

THE CONGREGATIONAL CHAPEL, built in 1817.

ST PETER'S CHURCH SCHOOL at the bottom of Hyde Lane now houses the public library.

BURIAL WAS NOT EXPENSIVE in 1878.

The Old George Inn

THE OLD GEORGE INN, sketched by the Revd W.J. Vashon Baker. It stood at the end of George, otherwise Love, Lane and it is said Oliver Cromwell stayed there during the Great Rebellion. The site is now occupied by the Roman Catholic church, which Cromwell would certainly not have approved of.

THE MODERN ROMAN CATHOLIC CHURCH in George Lane.

THE OPENING OF THE NEW METHODIST CHURCH in June 1910. John Wesley preached in Marlborough in 1745 and 1747. The site of the church was bought in 1816 and the church extended in 1842.

Municipal Matters

Before 1974 Marlborough had a long history of running its own affairs, dating from a charter granted by King John in 1204 to its leading citizens. By the seventeenth century it had a Corporation consisting of a self-electing Mayor, Aldermen and Burgesses, and the right (which it had acquired in the thirteenth century) to send two members to Parliament. Mere residence within the borough's bounds gave no automatic right to vote for MPs or Burgesses, the latter – some one hundred in the early eighteenth century, declining to only ten or so by 1800 – jealously guarding that privilege. Such a close Corporation was by the latter date an obvious target for the reforming Whig party. The Corporation was proud of its town, however, and following a disastrous fire in 1653, which destroyed most of the houses in the High Street, successively built three town halls, ran a successful grammar school, organized the markets, had its own fire brigade, magistrates and lock-up, and supported the parish church, as well as the poor and other worthy objects. These rights and powers were gradually eroded in the Victorian era. Nowadays the Mayor and Corporation only have the function of a parish council.

THE TOWN HALL or Market House, built after the fire of 1653. The ground floor was an open arcade for the sale of farm produce, particularly cheese. The Corporation met on the floors above.

THE SAME, from a print of 1793.

THE SECOND TOWN HALL, built in 1793. The ground floor is partly enclosed at the back. The pinnacles on St Mary's church have been removed.

MARKET HOUSE in 1822. The building was reconstructed in 1867.

THE BURGESSES improved the Town Hall
on the same site in 1867.

THE NORTH SIDE of the mid-
Victorian Town Hall.

THE MAURICES OF MARLBOROUGH c. 1904. A distinguished medical family. Dr J.B. Maurice, his wife, ten sons and two (of three) daughters. Members of the family have held mayoral office on ten occasions.

THE PRESENT TOWN HALL, by C.E. Ponting FSA, was opened in 1902.

THE MAYOR, Dr W.B. Maurice MBE, with councillors and officers in 1912.

THE MAYOR with Field Marshall Lord Methuen. Dr Maurice is fourth from the Mayor's right in the top hat.

THE MAYOR OF MARLBOROUGH
(COUNCILLOR THOMAS FREE, J.P.)
Wearing the New Mayoral Chain and Gown.

SUPPLEMENT TO THE "WILTS, BERKS AND HANTS COUNTY PAPER," DEC. 18TH, 1913.

COUNCILLOR THOMAS FREE JP, in mayoral robes, 1911. He was responsible for planting the trees on the Rockley Road.

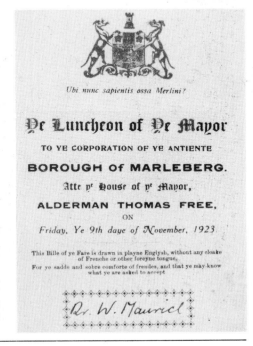

Ubi nunc sapientis ossa Merlini?

Ye Luncheon of Ye Mayor

TO YE CORPORATION OF YE ANTIENTE

BOROUGH of MARLEBERG.

Atte ye House of ye Mayor,

ALDERMAN THOMAS FREE,

ON

Friday, Ye 9th daye of November, 1923.

This Bille of ye Fare is drawn in playne Englysh, without any cloake of Frenche or other foreyne tongue,
For ye sadde and sobre comforts of frendes, and that ye may know what ye are asked to accept

R. W. Maurice

THE MAYOR'S LUNCHEON INVITATION of 1923. Alderman Thomas Free OBE was Mayor of Marlborough six times; his son Alderman E.J. Free MBE held the same office on five occasions.

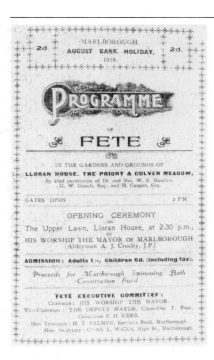

A MAYORAL OCCASION held in a good cause.

PRIDE IN THE ANCIENT BOROUGH is combined with a sense of fun. This was the menu for 5 November 1898 when Dr J.B. Maurice was about to complete his fourth mayoral term of office.

Þe Bille of yᵉ Fare.

Yᵉ Anchovies from yᵉ Countrie of Norwaye.

Yᵉ Olive from yᵉ French Countrie to provoke yᵉ appetyte.

Clear Soupe made wyth yᵉ younge Vegetables,
& also yᵉ deceivynge Turtle.

Yᵉ Smeltes fryed.

Yᵉ Turbotte boyled & served wyth yᵉ sauce of Lobstere.

Beef fillets wyth yᵉ Mushrooms of yᵉ Faery Ringe added thereunto.

Mutton Cutlets wyth yᵉ Love Apple.

Yᵉ Creams made wyth yᵉ fleshe of yᵉ Fowle.

Yᵉ Haunche of yᵉ Bucke from yᵉ Forest of Savernake.

Yᵉ Turkie boyled & yᵉ Tongue of yᵉ younge Ox.

Yᵉ English Wylde Duck & yᵉ Pheasant of Asia.

Yᵉ antiente Hamme from yᵉ Citie of Yorke.

Jellies wyth divers Fruites thereinne.

Curyous Pastryes.

Pudynges frozen inne ice after yᵉ Nesselrode mannere.

Divers Fruytes wʰ are your Desertes, & yᵉ Wynes of Champagne & manie outlandysh Countrees.

Yᵉ Dinner will be served after yᵉ mannere of yᵉ Russian People
Yᵉ Guestes are bidden to eate after yᵉ Hungarie mannere.

Þe Soupe.

Þe Fisshe.

Fleshe & Fowle.

Þe Fruytes, etc.

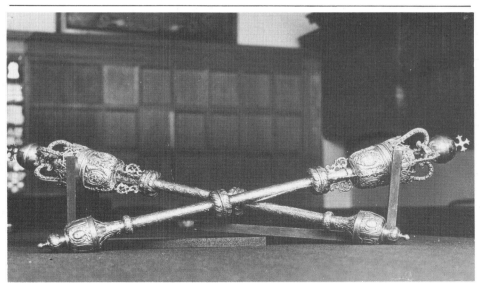

THE BOROUGH had particularly fine maces for ceremonial occasions as early as 1548. These were bought in 1652 at a cost of £45 8s. and are still used today.

At a Meeting of the Town Council held at the Guildhall on Tuesday the 17th of February, 1863,

It was determined to recommend, for the Celebration of

THE MARRIAGE

OF HIS ROYAL HIGHNESS

THE PRINCE OF WALES,

That the Mayor should request that all Shops shall be closed, and Business suspended as far as practicable. And that a treat of Tea and Cake be given to the Children of the several Day and Sunday Schools in the Town. And that there be a general Ball, at a moderate price for admission, in the Evening.

Such of the Inhabitants as are willing to subscribe to this object, and to form a Committee for furthering it, are requested to meet a Committee of the Town Council, at the *Guildhall*, on Monday the 23rd instant, at 12 o'clock at noon.

[W. W. LUCY, PRINTER.]

D. P. MAURICE, Mayor.

AN OPPORTUNITY for the citizens of Marlborough to display their loyalty. The Prince of Wales, later King Edward VII, was marrying Princess Alexandra of Denmark.

TABLES AND BENCHES IN THE HIGH STREET for a town feast on the occasion of Queen Victoria's Jubilee in 1887. The Mayor and Corporation fostered such celebrations.

CELEBRATIONS FOR THE CORONATION OF EDWARD VII outside the Town Hall.

THE TOWN COUNCIL used the hexagonal building in the foreground as a lock-up and weighhouse; it was demolished in 1925. The print is from 1855.

MARLBOROUGH GRAMMAR SCHOOL, founded in 1550, has a distinguished history. It was rebuilt in the eighteenth century and in 1904.

MAINTAINING A FIRE BRIGADE was an important municipal activity. No doubt the councillors were aware of the town's history and of the disastrous fire in 1653, which destroyed most of the houses – then thatched – in the High Street. During the Second World War the fire brigade's engine was lent to London.

THE CORPORATION fostered the town band which played on such festive occasions as Mayor-making. This is an 1897 jubilee celebration outside the old Town Hall.

A MAYORAL OCCASION outside the new Town Hall, designed in 1882 but not built until 1900–2.

THE TOWN BAND IN THE HIGH STREET, 1910, for the coronation of George V.

JUDGING FROM THE LADIES' DRESSES and the soldiers in the foreground, this could be a recruiting meeting in 1914/15.

ANOTHER MAYORAL OCCASION. A lady appears to be in charge of the white horse and cab in the foreground.

WATERLOO HOUSE, the offices and printing works of the *Marlborough Times*, decorated for the coronation of King Edward VII in 1902. The staff are having a party. The building at 29 High Street has been demolished and the site is now a newsagent's.

THE PROCLAMATION OF KING GEORGE V by the Mayor, Alderman E.J. Hill in April 1910.

AN ARCHITECT'S DRAWING for the new Town Hall of 1902.

LONDON ROAD decorated for the coronation of King George V in 1910.

KING GEORGE VI AND QUEEN ELIZABETH acknowledge the plaudits of the loyal citizens of Marlborough from the balcony of the Town Hall in March 1948.

QUEEN ELIZABETH WATCHES KING GEORGE VI sign the Corporation's visitors' book.

COUNCILLOR JAMES DUCK, THE MAYOR, presenting Alderman F. Simons, mayor in 1919 and 1929, to His Majesty during the royal visit of 1948.

Transport

An octogenarian writing in 1915 of the coaching period said: 'Marlborough was full of coaches and the streets presented a very animated scene on their arrival and departure. With the advent of the railway the coaches went off the road and the scene when I visited it about twenty years later was in striking contrast ... No longer were coaches to be seen, the great road wagons, each with its hood, which used to carry goods, were all gone. So too were the yellow post-chaises and people posting up to Town ... The town appeared to be almost deserted, and but for the establishment of the College its fortunes would soon have been at a very low ebb ... With the advent of motors I have witnessed a wonderful revival of road traffic through Marlborough, and once again the streets are busy with through traffic, so the town is coming into its own again.' It has indeed, if the difficulty in parking on a weekday is anything to go by.

A GREAT WESTERN RAILWAY PUBLICITY POSTER of the 1930s. An artist's impression of the view from the top of Granham Hill.

A HAYWAIN passing Silbury Hill.

A STAGE-WAGON approaches Marlborough from the south. From a 1790 print by Robinson and Foulder.

A STAGE-WAGON by St Peter's church. Notice its broad wheels. The broader the wheels the lower the turnpike toll.

A STAGE-COACH outside the Old Swan Inn at 100 High Street, the Sun Inn beyond.

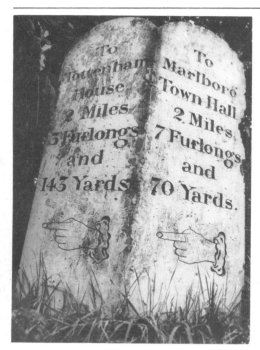

SHOWING THE WAY — milestones of the turnpike age. The one above may well have been promoted by the Earl of Ailesbury, who rebuilt Tottenham House in 1825.

THE ANGEL INN (now No. 8 High Street) had stabling for 300 horses in coaching days. It is the building on the right next but one to the Ailesbury Arms. The stables became cottages known as Angel Yard. The photograph is of about 1903.

A. BREWER, LANDLORD OF THE THREE TUNS, would provide neat post chaises for hire. At the height of the season forty coaches a day passed through the town. The inn closed in 1794.

MANY GATES REMAINED for the purpose of preventing cattle from straying long after the turnpike trusts disappeared in the nineteenth century. Small boys would earn pennies by opening them to traffic, of which there was very little after the coaches and before 1900.

AN EARLY ATTEMPT to apply steam to road transport. Ten of these were built. One steam carriage actually accomplished a journey from London to Bath via Marlborough.

BENJN GROBETY's

DEVIZES, CALNE, MARLBOROUGH,

NEWBURY, HUNGERFORD, RAMSBURY, &c. &c.

STAGE WAGGONS,

To and From the Swan-Inn, Holborn-Bridge, London,
every Monday, Tuesday, Wednesday, Thursday & Friday;
convey Goods to the Above and all adjacent Places.
Call at the OLD WHITE-HORSE CELLAR, & WHITE BEAR, PICCADILLY.
☞ No Money, Plate, Jewels, Glass, China, or any other Package, above the value of 5*l.*
will be accounted for, if lost or damaged, unless entered as such and paid for accordingly.
G. Hazard, Printer, 50, Beech-Street, London.

A TEAM OF EIGHT HORSES was necessary for these large waggons because of the bad state of the roads.

THE RAILWAY AGE. Lord Bruce is illustrated turning the first sod of the Swindon, Marlborough and Andover railway in 1875, which opened eight years later. Marlborough's first railway, in 1864, was only to Savernake.

THE HIGH- AND LOW-LEVEL STATIONS appear on this sketch of around 1910. The artist, P.C. Treen, has put his initials on the luggage roll in the foreground.

MARLBOROUGH LOW-LEVEL GWR SIGNAL BOX was opened in 1933. The horsebox bay for racehorse traffic on the right was closed in the late 1930s due to road traffic frightening horses. Shunters' Cottage is on the left.

A CHELTENHAM TO SOUTHAMPTON TRAIN at Marlborough in 1947. The GWR high-level station was only used for goods traffic after 1933. The Salisbury Road bridge is in the foreground, and the footpath to the station master's house is on the right.

THE LAST TRAIN TO ANDOVER, the 5.25, on the Midland and South Western line. The station closed on 9 September 1961.

THE GREAT WESTERN RAILWAY took over the Marlborough to Savernake line, and this service, connecting Calne and Marlborough stations, was started on 10 October 1904. It was operated initially by two 22-seat 20 hp Milne–Daimler buses. The service ceased on 26 July 1913, but was reintroduced by GWR in July 1924.

AN EARLY THORNEYCROFT BUS.

A HORSE OUTSIDE THE BEAR AND CASTLE enjoys its bag of oats in around 1890.

THE EMPTY ROAD of around 1900, before the college archway over the road was built in 1911.

THE TOWN STREETS WERE QUIET after the coaches had left and before the motors came. Sir Aston Webb's College arch is pictured with hansom cab and top-hatted driver, c. 1912. The arch was designed not to avoid the hazard of crossing the road but to connect Field House with the main school, the gates of which were locked at sundown.

THE SUN INN AND ST PETER'S CHURCH OF ENGLAND SCHOOL (now the public library) at the junction of High and Hyde Streets. No dog would venture a nap in the middle of the High Street nowadays.

A HANSOM CAB waits for a fare in the quiet High Street in around 1910.

AN EARLY CAR, C. 1905. The ladies wore veils to keep their hats on and the dust out.

A CAR RALLY outside the Ailesbury Arms, c. 1902. The landlord's card read, 'By appointment, headquarters of the Automobile Club'.

THE COMING OF THE MOTOR AGE. A constrast: Dr W.B. Maurice's car *and* carriage outside Lloran House in the High Street, *c.* 1900.

AN EARLY MARLBOROUGH HIGH STREET GARAGE, with petrol pump and a vehicle emerging (right).

THE HIGH STREET, c. 1920, looking towards St Peter's church, with only one car and one lorry in sight.

THE HIGH STREET begins to fill with cars and buses in around 1925.

OLD AND NEW. The prehistoric Silbury Hill forms the background to the twentieth-century service station and tea gardens. The former outlived the latter, and the National Trust now owns the site. The intrusion has been removed.

TRAFFIC IN THE HIGH STREET after the Second World War. There is still room to park.

THE HIGH STREET FILLS UP. One of the buses has two decks.

AN OUTING BY OPEN COACH, c. 1925.

THOMAS FREE'S FURNITURE VAN, pictured in around 1932, was a two-ton Ford.

Inns, Hotels and Trades

When the Castle Inn closed its mantle passed to the Ailesbury Arms, for long the leading hostelry until rivalled by the Castle and Ball. The Bear and Castle, opposite the Town Hall at No. 1 High Street, had a licence by 1757, and is now known as The Bear. The Angel at 8 High Street was an inn in 1605, a coffee tavern in 1883 and a temperance hotel until 1930. It is now offices. The Sun Inn by St Peter's at 90 High Street has an interesting interior and dates from 1751. The Five Alls at 13 London Road dates from 1780. At one time or another Marlborough has had some one hundred and fifty 'watering holes', and to walk from one end of the High Street to the other and have a modest pint at each of them between opening and closing time would not be easy today.

The most interesting feature of the town is the colonnading on the north side of the High Street which, except in the case of the Midland Bank at No. 141, has been well preserved when development has taken place. It is better to look at the pillars and canopies of the colonnade and the storeys above than at some of the shop-fronts.

THE CASTLE AND BALL HOTEL, the Antelope until 1763, at 117 High Street. The Old White Hart, where Shakespeare is said to have played, was next door.

THE BEAR HOTEL, formerly the Bear and Castle, at 1 High Street.

OLD WHITE HART YARD, from an etching of 1933 by Christopher Hughes.

THE AILESBURY ARMS, an inn for many years, acquired a leading position when the Castle Inn closed in the 1840s. It is now No. 6 High Street.

THE GARDEN BEHIND THE HOTEL, c. 1920. It has been developed as offices.

THE SUN INN has been at 90 High Street, the corner of Hyde Lane, since 1750. Elizabethan panelling remains. Lloran House is opposite.

THE FIVE ALLS in London Road, formerly known as The Marsh.

FREDK J. CHANDLER (Est. 1800), a noted leather and saddlery shop in London Road, about 1900.

THE FIRM WAS HONOURED by the grant of a royal warrant.

The
Polly Tea Rooms

Home-made Cakes and Chocolates.
Hot and Cold Luncheons and TEAS.

SUNDAYS—Open from 12.30 p.m.

27 HIGH STREET
MARLBOROUGH.

Telephone   MARLBOROUGH 146.

THE POLLY at 26–7 the High Street is now mostly one storey, following a serious fire in 1966. In the eighteenth century it had been known as the Half Moon.

THE POLLY BURNING IN 1966. Firemen George Johnson and Robert Cox received special commendations for rescuing children from the upper floor.

Marlboro' 14-6   Marlborough, Wilts.

And so to Bath . . .

"Since it is not yet the hour which we have appointed for meeting young Peter, who will conduct us over the School, and then take us to the right tea-shop", we will turn in at St. Peter's Church, closing in the High Street, opposite the School," . . . . I thought what a good walk it made as Peter took me off to tea after viewing the Chapel, with it's panels bearing the names of distinguished old boys, and its frescoes showing the influence of another O.M.—William Morris.

"Actually we shall see the boys of Marlborough College coming out of . . . . . Polly's tea-rooms with their 'people'."

The tea-shop was full of youth and noise. It stood in the High Street by an archway that had once led into a coachyard . . . . . It being six o'clock, the College curfew imminent, Peter rose from the table. . . . . . But I lingered in Polly's Tea Shop, by the bow-window commanding a view of the old street.

"And so to Bath"

Reproduced with the consent of the publishers, Hodder & Stoughton, London, from the book by Cecil Roberts.

THE POLLY'S MODEST ADVERTISEMENT, c. 1900.

LUCY AND CO. at 132 High Street, were well-established printers in the last century.

THE INTERIOR. The house escaped the fire of 1653, and the fine oak panelling was preserved.

NO. 125 HIGH STREET. The three-gabled house was pulled down in 1868 and Lloyds Bank now occupies the site.

ANTIQUE SHOPS were established early in Marlborough. This one stood on the north side of the High Street and is now the site of the White Horse bookshop.

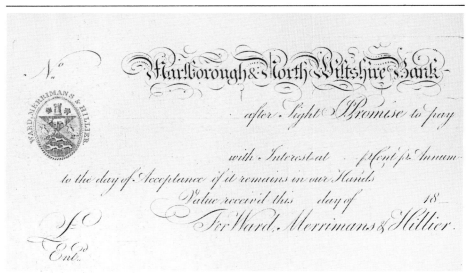

THE MARLBOROUGH AND NORTH WILTSHIRE BANK was absorbed by Capital and Counties Bank, and that in turn by Lloyds. Merrimans, long established solicitors, and Hillier are well-known Marlborough names.

The Capital and Counties Bank, Ltd.

Marlboro' Branch.

5 10 189 8

The Manager begs to acknowledge the receipt of your letter of ....with enclosures as therein stated, *for which he is obliged.—*

Exd.

H.P.S., LTD., 123,000—3-98.

JEEVES AND SONS were good butchers in extensive business in the 1920s.

BURNING PIGS' BRISTLES.

SHEEP RAISING ON THE MARLBOROUGH DOWNS played a large part in the local scene. Markets were first held on the Green and later on the Common.

PLOUGHING BY OXEN lasted until the turn of the century.

WATER MEADOWS AT PRESHUTE on the banks of the Kennet were important for grazing in early spring.

THE OLD SMITHY IN GEORGE LANE stood next to the Elizabethan cottages which still exist.

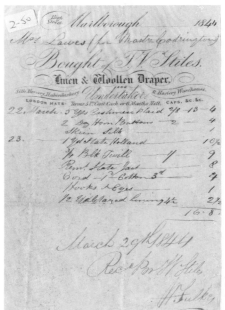

ON 23 AUGUST 1843, 200 Marlburians arrived at
the new school. This shows purchases for a boy
at the college when it first opened.

IRONMONGERS on the north side of the High
Street, c. 1900.

THE BELL AND SHOULDER OF MUTTON INN (1780–1952) at 44 Kingsbury Street.

THE AGRICULTURAL STAFF at Manton Farm, c. 1890. In 1877 the Mayor, Mr D.P. Maurice, entertained Mr Gladstone at Manton Grange.

THE FORMER GEORGE INN at 7 High Street. The occasion is the Coronation of George V. The Electricity Board occupies the site nowadays.

War: Preparation and Aftermath

Marlborough has many military connections. By Queen Victoria's reign, the town was running its own small force of volunteer infantry. The college did not lag behind the town, having its own corps of Rifle Volunteers by the 1880s, and the Grammar School had its own cadet company shortly after. The County Yeomanry Cavalry had its headquarters in Marlborough. The wide High Street was used for parades and inspections. Patriotism was strong in 1914, and the 7th Battalion, Wiltshire Regiment was recruited here. The college honoured its dead by the Memorial Hall, opened by the Duke of Connaught in 1925. Royalty visited the town in 1943 and 1948.

CAR INSPECTION following manoeuvres in September 1903 by Field Marshal Earl Roberts of Kandahar VC, in front of what is now Lloyds Bank.

OFFICERS OF THE WILTSHIRE YEOMANRY, C. 1890. Dr W.B. Maurice was its surgeon for thirty-two years. Early in the last century the Yeomanry were not always popular. For example:

> Then behold with contempt, and rejoice you're exempt
> From such an inglorious train,
> Whom folly may laud, and despots applaud,
> But Mars and the Muses disdain.

LIKE THE TOWN, the college had its own corps of Rifle Volunteers. This is the inspection of 27 May 1881 (from a coloured print in possession of the college).

GENERAL SIR IAN HAMILTON opens a miniature rifle range for Marlborough Grammar School in 1907.

ARMY VETERANS ON PARADE, Empire Day, 1913. The county was alarmed by German militarism.

MARLBOROUGH DETACHMENT OF ROYAL ENGINEERS exhibiting their steam engines and motor cycles, c. 1912.

THE 7TH BATTALION, WILTSHIRE REGIMENT recruited in Marlborough during the First World War.

THE BATTALION outside the Town Hall.

THE 7TH WILTSHIRES ON PARADE outside the Town Hall during the First World War.

THE BOY SCOUTS also paraded.

THE WIDE HIGH STREET used as a military transport park during the First World War.

AN AMBULANCE OUTSIDE THE TOWN HALL bought with money subscribed by the town.

A GIFT OF AMBULANCES by an Indian maharajah during the First World War.

COMFORT FOR THE FIRST WORLD WAR TROOPS: a good supper.

A CONCERT PARTY for the troops by local Marlburians.

VOLUNTEER STRETCHER BEARERS, probably from the staff of the college, outside the Priory (then a college boarding house and now an old peoples' home).

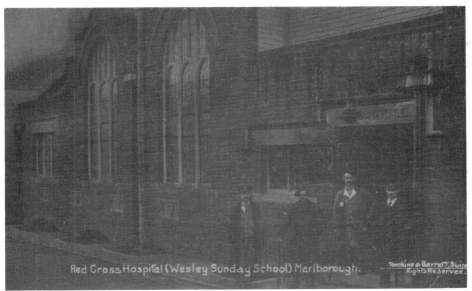

Red Cross Hospital (Wesley Sunday School) Marlborough.

THE WESLEY SUNDAY SCHOOL becomes a Red Cross hospital.

The Green (shewing fringe of Savernake Forest), Marlborough

AN ARMY UNIT ON THE GREEN at the time of the First World War.

PEACE CELEBRATIONS, July 1919. The Mayor is F. Simons.

UNVEILING OF THE WAR MEMORIAL to the dead of the 7th Wiltshire Regiment in 1919, by Field Marshal Lord Methuen of Corsham, distinguished soldier and Governor of Malta, 1915–19.

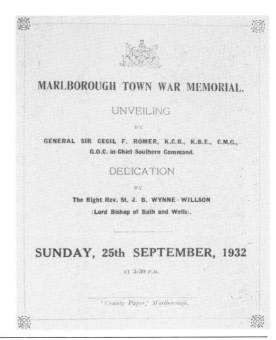

MARLBOROUGH TOWN WAR MEMORIAL.

UNVEILING

BY

GENERAL SIR CECIL F. ROMER, K.C.B., K.B.E., C.M.G., G.O.C.-in-Chief Southern Command.

DEDICATION

BY

The Right Rev. St. J. B. WYNNE-WILLSON (Lord Bishop of Bath and Wells).

SUNDAY, 25th SEPTEMBER, 1932

AT 3-30 P.M.

'County Paper,' Marlborough.

UNVEILING OF THE TOWN WAR MEMORIAL in 1932, fourteen years after the end of the First World War. Its original position was on a wall of the Town Hall.

J. Shirley-Fox
Marlborough
Sept 4. 1914

WILTSHIREMEN

England may not be a military nation in the modern sense of the word but she knows how to maintain her position as mistress of the world when called upon to do so and she intends to hold the heritage given to her by her ancestors and to hand it down even greater and stronger than she received it to her children

Methuen

FIELD MARSHAL LORD METHUEN GCB, GCMG, GCVO, a distinguished soldier of the Scots Guards. He was sixty when he wrote the patriotic message above.

THE WAR MEMORIAL STEPS from the college chapel to a garden of remembrance and the Memorial Hall from an etching by G.N. Holman. On a stone outside one may read, 'Let us make earth a garden in which the deeds of the valiant may blossom and bear fruit.'

THE MEMORIAL HALL AT THE COLLEGE, showing steps and garden. The hall was opened by the Duke of Connaught in 1925.

INTERIOR OF THE MEMORIAL HALL. Regrettably the names of some of those killed are now obscured by seating.

THE WINTER OF 1939/40 was particularly severe. Second World War troops clear snow on the Common, which was used by various army units including, later, the US Army.

WHITE HELL. The effect of the snow and ice in Hyde Lane.

HOME GUARD PLATOON formed from senior boys at the college in 1940.

REGIMENTAL SGT MAJOR J. BRAIN of the College Cadet Corps, and his family, outside Buckingham Palace when he was invested with the George Medal for gallantry in uncoupling ammunition wagons in Savernake Forest when fire made an explosion likely.

City of London School.

BILLET RULES

1. TIMES.

SENIORS (14 years or over) except Prefects and Sub-Prefects:

In billets by 8 p.m.

Lights out 10 p.m.

(A limited number of VI. Form boys may need to work late. They must have the written permission of their Form Master.)

JUNIORS (under 14 years):

In billets by 7 p.m.

(On Tuesday, Thursday, Saturday when tea is at 6.30, and on Sunday when tea is at 6.45, juniors must return to their billets immediately after tea.)

Lights out by 9 p.m. at latest.

(Young boys are expected to go to bed earlier at the discretion of the hostess.)

2. RETURNING TO BILLETS.

(a) Facilities are provided at the College for games, reading, writing, etc., and no boys need return to their billets in the morning except possibly to change for games.

They are forbidden to return except with the full approval of their hostesses, who are asked to let the Visiting Master know at once if this rule is broken.

(b) It is possible for nearly all boys to do preparation at school till 6.30 on Monday, Wednesday and Friday evenings if it is inconvenient for them to return to their billets earlier.

(c) No boy may visit another billet at any time except with the permission of the hostess in the house where the visit is made.

Sixth Form boys are allowed to visit another billet for work with another boy if the hostesses agree and if the Visiting Master has given written permission stating address and times.

Boys are not allowed to visit houses at any time where no boys or masters are billeted, except with the Visiting Master's written permission.

3. MEALS.

Meals are provided in College for all except Day Boys.

Hostesses are not asked to provide more than a hot drink, morning and evening, except when special arrangements have been made with parents.

4. GENERAL.

Boys are expected to look after themselves as much as possible. They should clean their own shoes and keep their rooms tidy.

They are expected to do what is asked of them in the houses in which they live. In bad weather they should change their outdoor shoes immediately they return.

It is important that boys should never miss Assembly at 8, or breakfast on Saturday or Sunday, unless they are sick. In case of sickness, a visit will be made without delay. If they are not visited, hostesses are asked to let the Visiting Master or the School Office at the College Tel. M. 367, know as soon as they can.

Smoking is not allowed in billets or anywhere else in term time. The Cinema is out of bounds.

Any complaints should be made to the Visiting Master as quickly as possible.

F. R. DALE,
Headmaster.

Visiting Master......*J. N. Wheeler*..............

Address......*The Red House Cardigan Rd*

MARLBOROUGH, 1940.

IN 1940 when heavy bombing of London was anticipated, the college opened its doors to receive 700 boys of the City of London School. They were billeted in the town. The college and school 'boxed and coxed' for use of the classrooms.

QUEEN ELIZABETH (now the Queen Mother) reviews the Queen's Bays (2nd Dragoon Guards) in 1941 on the college cricket field.

THE POET CHARLES HAMILTON SORLEY at an Officers Training Corps camp (seated, barefooted), and as a young officer. He was killed in 1915, aged twenty. He wrote from France,

Crouched where the open upland billows down
   Into the valley where the river flows,
She is as any other country town,
   That little lives or marks or hears or knows.

And she can teach but little. She has not
   The wonder and the surging and the roar
Of striving cities. Only things forgot
   That once were beautiful, but now no more

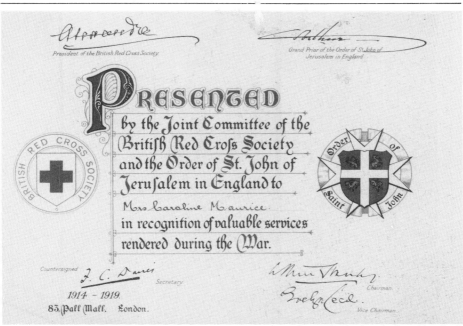

President of the British Red Cross Society

Grand Prior of the Order of St John of Jerusalem in England

PRESENTED

by the Joint Committee of the British Red Cross Society and the Order of St. John of Jerusalem in England to

Mrs Caroline Maurice

in recognition of valuable services rendered during the War.

Countersigned *J. C. Davis*
Secretary

Chairman

Vice Chairman

1914 – 1919.
83. Pall Mall. London.

IN BOTH WORLD WARS civilians played a conspicuous part in 'keeping the home fires burning'. Here Queen Alexandra expresses appreciation for work in the First World War and, below, Queen Elizabeth for the Second World War.

I WISH TO MARK, BY THIS PERSONAL MESSAGE, my appreciation of the service you have rendered to your Country in 1939. In the early days of the War you opened your door to strangers who were in need of shelter, & offered to share your home with them. I know that to this unselfish task you have sacrificed much of your own comfort, & that it could not have been achieved without the loyal co-operation of all in your household. By your sympathy you have earned the gratitude of those to whom you have shown hospitality, & by your readiness to serve you have helped the State in a work of great value.

Elizabeth R

IN MARCH 1948 King George VI honoured the Borough and college by a visit. Here he inspects the guard of honour of the Army and Sea Cadets of the college, accompanied by the Master, Mr M.F. Heywood.

THE ROYAL VISIT TO MARLBOROUGH COLLEGE. The Master presents Captain G.W.B. Hext RN (Retd), the bursar. Captain Hext was a midshipman with the king.

THE KING AND QUEEN with the Master, Viscount Jowitt the Lord Chancellor, and Dr Fisher, Archbishop of Canterbury, the College Visitor.

GB 14 43 bc Geheim	Marlborough Zeltlager	Karte 1:100 000 Engl. Bl. 33 a
Bild Nr. 372 Z 14	Geogr. Lage 1°44' W, 51°26' N, Höhe ü. d. M. 180 m	Stand VIII 4
	Maßstab etwa 1:10 000 (1 cm = 160 m)	

(A)   GB 14 43 Zeltlager M a r l b o r o u g h
ca. 25 Langzelte
ca. 90 Rundzelte

AERIAL PHOTOGRAPH OF
~ MARLBOROUGH ~

THE ORIGINAL OF THIS PHOTOGRAPH hangs in the Mayor's Parlour at the Town Hall and is reproduced by courtesy of the Mayor of Marlborough. August 1940 was the time of the Battle of Britain, the German attempt to defeat the Royal Air Force and then invade the country. The German bomber was probably making for the Swindon railway yards, with Marlborough Common, where tanks were located, as a secondary target.

142

Recreation

Before the days of the cinema, radio and television, the citizen largely made his or her own pleasure in village games, such as quoits, or picnics for example – and welcomed the periodical fairs, with their novelties and cheerful bustle. Team games, essentially cricket and football, played a good part in village and small town life, and received much impetus from the public schools. Cycling clubs were popular and both sexes could participate. By 1910 the Boy Scout movement was well established, albeit slightly tinged with militarism, so that the local Scout troops paraded on Empire Day 1913 with the veterans of the National Reserve which, strangely, the War Office forbade the Officers Training Corps at Marlborough College to do. Bonfires and ox-roasting took place on occasions of public rejoicing, such as coronations and royal jubilees.

THE MOP FAIRS IN THE 1920S. Little and Big Mop originated as small hiring occasions. A farm labourer would advertise his availability by putting corn in his hat; a maid servant would carry a mop – and so the term 'Mop Fair' came into use. Held on the Saturdays before and after 11 October each year, these events now claim to be the largest street fairs in the West Country, and are totally transformed into fun fairs.

BOYS OF MARLBOROUGH GRAMMAR SCHOOL in Savernake Forest with peashooters and catapults after a squirrel, c. 1860.

BOYS OF MARLBOROUGH COLLEGE play at elementary hockey by the College gates.

MARLBOROUGH COLLEGE CRICKET TEAM before the pavilion in 1856.

THE COLLEGE ELEVEN in 1862.

THE MATCH BETWEEN THE COLLEGE AND MASTERS in 1860. Both players and spectators are posing for the camera. The masters, who are batting, obviously differed in opinion as to the correct dress. Note the White Horse on the Down, and the tower of St Peter's church.

PEWSEY VALE CYCLING CLUB. President's run to Marlborough, 24 August 1898.

MARLBOROUGH TOWN'S QUOITS TEAM, C. 1900.

THE SCOUTS PARADE ON EMPIRE DAY 1913, complete with their own band. Scouting was very popular in Marlborough from the movement's beginning.

A MOP FAIR IN THE 1920s fills the whole High Street.

QUEEN VICTORIA'S JUBILEE, 1887. An ox-roasting in the High Street outside the Castle and Ball Hotel.

THE HIGH STREET decorated for the 1877 Jubilee.

THIS MAGNIFICENT BONFIRE on the Common was to celebrate the Coronation of George V. In the foreground is the Mayor, Thomas Free OBE, six times Mayor of Marlborough.

DR WALTER MAURICE MBE, County Commissioner of the Boy Scouts and Mayor of Marlborough in 1912. He was awarded the Silver Wolf Badge, the Scouts' highest honour.

E.G.H. KEMPSON (left), naturalist, archaeologist, mountaineer and scholar, taught at Marlborough College from 1925 to 1967 and was Mayor of Marlborough in 1947. He is seen here with two colleagues of the Everest Expedition of 1935 and 1936.

THE COLLEGE BATHING PLACE in what remains of the castle moat.

SKATING IN THE COLLEGE COURT after the great ice storm of January 1940, known as 'white hell'. A postman skated along the Bath Road to deliver mail, and ice-bound steps meant that Dr T.K. Maurice had to crawl to see a patient.

DR J.W. IVIMEY CONDUCTING the college orchestra after the opening of the College Memorial Hall in 1925.

A PARTY FOR SCOUTS in the grounds of Lloran House, home of Dr Walter B. Maurice, County Commissioner.

THE RT HON. WALTER LONG MP and Dr Maurice with the Parade Marshal on Empire Day 1913, when the Scouts paraded with the veterans of the National Reserve.

QUEEN ELIZABETH, THE QUEEN MOTHER, accepts a sausage cooked by the Scouts at Marlborough College in 1948.

A PICNIC FOR THE MAURICE FAMILY, doctors in Marlborough for the last 198 years. This is from around 1880.

PONY AND TRAP. The photograph, of about 1914, is by J.J. Hunt of 25a Kingsbury Street, Marlborough.

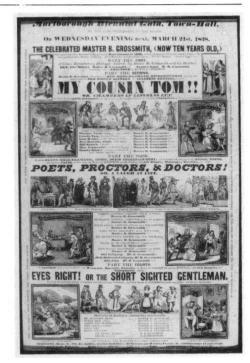

TWO PIECES OF LIGHT-HEARTED FRIVOLITY.

Malbrough s'en va-t'en guerre !

ACKNOWLEDGEMENTS

The pleasure of collecting these photographs has been made the greater by the very willing assistance of Dr Tim Maurice, Mr David West, archivist of Marlborough College, and of Mrs West. In particular I must thank my friend and mentor Group Captain Stephen Beaumont for supplying me with so many ideas when inspiration was lacking and for always being there to offer advice and encouragement, David Hyde, who offered treasured photographs for the railways section, and R.C. Riley and P.J. Garland.

The following helped me in various ways or lent, and gave me permission to reproduce, photographs:

The Mayor and Town Clerk of Marlborough • Wiltshire Archaeological and Natural History Society • Merrimans, Solicitors • The Polly Tea Rooms Wiltshire County Council • The Great Barn, Avebury • The Bodleian Library Sheila Follet • Roger Pope • Mrs Mary Siggers • Mrs Margaret Kempson Michael Gray • Dick Maurice • John and Michael O'Regan • David Chandler Christopher Sykes • David Hyde • Kenneth Hillier • Peter Treloar Peter Daniels

My sincere thanks to each and every one, and my apologies for any omissions or errors which may have crept in at the last minute. The responsibility is entirely mine. The copying of the original photographs has been undertaken by Derek Parker.